Advent
Adventure

Advent ┐
└Adventure

A stimulating study course for Advent

CLARE & HUBERT RICHARDS

First published in 2000 by
KEVIN MAYHEW LTD
Buxhall
Stowmarket
Suffolk IP14 3BW

0 1 2 3 4 5 6 7 8 9

ISBN 1 84003 619 2
Catalogue No 1500382

Cover design by Jonathan Stroulger
Typesetting by Richard Weaver
Printed and bound in Great Britain

Foreword

We have written this book together, to offer groups or individuals some food for thought during Advent. The four sections are based on the Gospel readings for the four Sundays of Advent. We have selected a predominant theme from each Gospel and explored it in several ways.

- A brief commentary on the Gospel text by Bert

- Further thoughts taken from everyday life by Clare

- A short selection of quotations on the theme

- Some questions for discussion

Clare wrote the introduction and conclusion.

The Gospel quotations are from the Jerusalem Bible and the New Jerusalem Bible.

Acknowledgements

The publishers wish to express their gratitude to the following copyright owners who have granted permission to include their copyright material in this book.

Rev J. Badcock, for his text, *A Dissenter's Hail Mary*.

Darton, Longman & Todd Ltd, 1 Spencer Court, 140-142 Wandsworth High Street, London, SW18 4JJ, for extracts taken from the *Jerusalem Bible*, published and copyright 1966, 1967 and 1968 by Darton, Longman & Todd Ltd and Doubleday & Co Inc, and the *New Jerusalem Bible*, published and copyright 1985 by Darton, Longman & Todd Ltd and les Editions du Cerf, and used by permission of the publishers.

McCrimmons Publishing Co Ltd, 10-12 High Street, Great Wakering, Southend-on-Sea, Essex, SS3 0EQ, for extracts taken from *Pilgrim to the Holy Land*, © McCrimmon Publishing Co Ltd.

Archbishop Cormac Murphy O'Connor for the extract from his address when he was installed as Archbishop of Westminster.

Every effort has been made to trace the owners of copyright material, and we hope that no copyright has been infringed. Pardon is sought and apology made if the contrary be the case, and a correction will be made in any reprint of this book.

Contents

Introduction

I love these busy weeks before Christmas, preparing for the event. I know that many Christians regret the commercial Christmas, the secular celebration that seems to be taking over. And I do regret parts of it. But I can't say I get too upset by the hustle and bustle, the cooking, the colourful shops and the lists of presents, and the thousand and one things to do in the next few weeks.

I remember my distinct discomfort in church one Advent Sunday, years ago, when the children were small and the thought of Christmas was all excitement and secrets. The priest bewailed commercial Christmases and busy preparations, saying that the birth of Jesus was a quiet, peaceful event for Mary and Joseph, and we needed to imitate their calm prayerfulness.

Get real, I thought. Mary was having a baby, for heaven's sake, with all the pain, anxiety, disruption that childbirth inevitably causes. The story even speaks of the couple as homeless refugees. Fat chance for a peaceful delivery! I imagine Mary would have been frantic with worry and last-minute, unexpected preparations.

What are we actually celebrating, then, at Christmas? Surely the fundamental fact that the mysterious God is not too distant to be understood. We celebrate in the very ordinary birth of this baby the fact that God can be known and touched in the most human of events. God is present with us in our human lives. We mistake the Christian mystery of Incarnation if we think God can only be found amongst the angels, in churches or in heaven.

I want to find God in the frantic Christmas rush, in the tinsel-decorated shops, in the impossible queues, and in the staff parties. Don't you? Maybe, however, the priest in his sermon was warning us that we need moments of calm too, lest we fail to see the wood for the Christmas trees. So perhaps his sermon did have a point after all.

I hope this book will offer you a little food for thought – to aid your *quiet* preparation for Christmas.

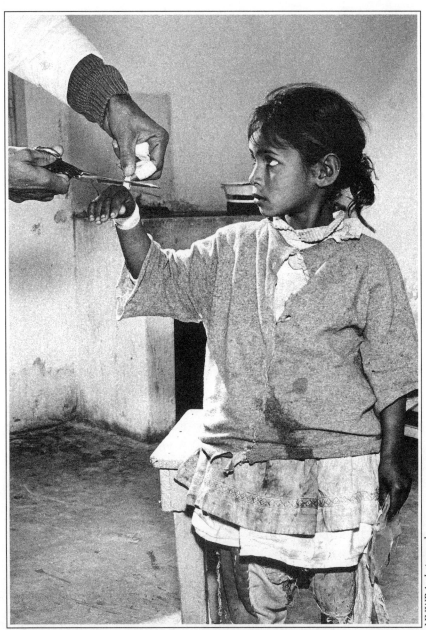

Ours are the only hands God has

Week One _____

_____ *Liberation*

Reading for the first Sunday of Advent

Jesus said to his disciples: 'There will be signs in the sun and moon and stars; on earth nations in agony, bewildered by the clamour of the ocean and its waves; men dying of fear as they await what menaces the world, for the powers of heaven will be shaken. And then they will see the Son of Man coming in a cloud with power and great glory. When these things begin to take place, stand erect, **hold your heads high, because your liberation is near at hand.**'
Luke 21:25-28

It's a confusing time, this month running up to Christmas.
We call these four weeks 'Advent' – a Latin word meaning 'arriving' or 'coming'.
What we're talking about, of course, is the arrival of Christ, the coming into the world of Jesus at Christmas.
Advent is a time for looking forward to that day.

Looking forward?
Isn't it rather odd to look forward to something that happened in the past?
How can you long for something to come when it's already history –
two-thousand-years-ago history, and getting further and further away as the years go on?
Isn't this simply a childish game of make-believe?

Yes, it's true.
We *are* playing a sort of game over these weeks of Advent.
But it's not childish.
There's a deadly serious purpose behind this game.

Just think.

Have you ever wondered why the Jews, every spring, year in and year out, celebrate their feast of Passover, and make believe they're still making their way to the Promised Land?

That happened over three thousand years ago!

That's true. But the real Promised Land they're longing for still remains in the future.

Have you ever wondered why the Americans, every autumn, year in, year out, still celebrate Thanksgiving Day, and make believe they've only just arrived in the Land of the Free?

That happened nearly four hundred years ago!

That's true. But the universal freedom they're longing for still remains in the future.

Have you ever wondered why here in Great Britain, every November, year in, year out, we solemnly celebrate the end of two World Wars, and make believe it's happening now?

When it actually happened two generations ago!

That's true. But the perfect peace we're all longing for still lies in the future.

In other words, there's a very serious purpose behind the make-believe we're all playing.

We look back behind us like a farmer ploughing a furrow, to make sure we're keeping in the right direction ahead.

And we Christians, year in and year out, do the same thing every Advent.

Yes, it's true that it's two thousand years since God sent Jesus into our unfree world, to liberate us, to set us free.

And, yes, it's true, he showed us the direction we must look if the freedom he brought us was to be kept safe.

But just look at the daily paper and read about it, whether it's in Kosovo or Chechnya or Mozambique, or nearer home in our own cities and villages – the unfreedom that still shackles so many people in this rich world of poor people.

That's why we take time off every Advent to listen again to these words of Jesus: 'Hold your head high! Liberation! It's near at hand! Can you feel it?'

That it will come is certain: God has promised it, and we can be confident that it's all in his hands.

Can we still feel as confident when we realise that ours are the only hands God has?

Because that's part of what Advent is about too, as we shall see.

Our Father who art in heaven,
thy kingdom come,
and deliver us from evil.

Hold your head high because your liberation is near at hand.

What does it mean to be free?

As Jesus was approaching his final Passover he spoke the encouraging words, 'Hold your head high because your liberation is near at hand.'

What did he mean? Liberation from what? Liberation for what?

The words imply that people were held in some kind of bondage. The immediate reaction of his friends would have been mixed. Some probably thought he was referring to the Roman occupation of Palestine, and would have been delighted at the thought of an unoccupied homeland at last. But close friends would have known by then that Jesus was not speaking of contemporary political situations. His preaching had been quite consistent. He only had eyes for the kingdom of God. He was referring to a freedom of spirit that would allow people to follow God's Rule rather than their own selfish or sinful ways. Everything Jesus preached was really about freedom.

Sin keeps people in bondage.
Injustice keeps people in bondage.
Blindness keeps people in bondage.
Poverty keeps people in bondage.
Inability to forgive keeps people in bondage.
Lack of compassion keeps people in bondage.
Prejudice keeps people in bondage.
Love of power keeps people in bondage.

And all these things keep people from recognising the kingdom of God – here and now, on earth. Jesus never forced anyone to accept this truth. After all, he respected their freedom. He offered the invitation to follow his Way, which was God's Way. When I was teaching RE I used to sum up Jesus' teaching as LFC – Love, Forgiveness and Compassion. (This made it easy to recall as it reminded us of LFC – Liverpool Football Club.) We always concluded, on looking closely at these values, that a loving, forgiving, compassionate person was truly free.

Take an example. Look at the contrast between the sad, tragic figure of the mother of Lesley-Ann Downey (the child murdered by Brady and Hindley) and the generous Gordon Wilson whose daughter Marie was killed in the Enniskillen bombing. Lesley-Ann's mother was very understandably unable to forgive, but it utterly destroyed her. Over the years the poor woman became a pathetic, wounded figure, eaten up by her anger and distress. How could anyone blame her? Gordon Wilson lost his beloved daughter too, but to everyone's amazement his first words were of forgiveness, and he never lost his acceptance of the tragedy. And he used it as a way of seeking peace in Northern Ireland. His ability to forgive gave him a freedom to go on living in compassion and love.

So we have our answer to the question, *Liberation from what?* Liberation from everything that prevents us being loving, forgiving and compassionate people.

And we have our answer to the question, *Liberation for what?* Liberation for the sake of the kingdom of God. This means that a loving, forgiving and compassionate person brings the kingdom of God into being here and now.

In March 1964 a group of young theologians met at Petrópolis in Brazil to look again at the Christian Gospel in the context of the terrible poverty and suffering of their people. Four years later the bishops of Latin America took up this challenge at a meeting in Medellin, Colombia. They went on to denounce 'institutionalised' violence and injustice in much of the Third World. They pledged to work for the liberation of its victims, seeing this as a legitimate interpretation of Jesus' teaching. This was the beginning of a new way of understanding God and his kingdom, and is called Liberation Theology. In time it inspired the whole Church to consider taking the 'option for the poor'. Liberation from poverty is seen as an anticipation of what is to come.

One of the liberation theologians, Gustavo Gutierrez, described how peace, love, justice and freedom, which all involve relationships between people, are signs of the kingdom. He explains that:

(i) in so far as bringing about peace and justice depends on us, the kingdom is to be worked for.

(ii) in so far as its coming is ultimately God's work, it should be awaited in hope.

Liberation theologians base their thinking on the repeated insistence in the Bible that God is on the side of the poor and always seeks their freedom. They show, especially from Luke's Gospel, that Jesus made an 'option for the poor' and defended the outcasts. This means that following the Gospel implies social and political involvement. Gutierrez points out that sin is not a private reality. It has a collective dimension which results in people being oppressed, exploited and dominated by unjust governments.

This theology is clearly a move away from traditional European theology, which has always tended to 'privatise' the Christian message. Liberation theologians say that the older theology concentrated on the inner spiritual life of the individual and was more concerned with doctrine than with action.

This has made some Christians uneasy with liberation theology. They suspect it moves away from the Gospel by becoming too 'worldy' and political. They too can quote the Gospel. Jesus was clearly not disturbed by his contemporary political situation. He didn't enter into the politics of Roman occupation.

However, one thing is certain – this disagreement between theologians forces each one of us to look at our own faith to discover where we stand. What do I need to be liberated from? What did Jesus liberate me from?

Many years ago, when I was a student, I was given an essay title, 'How free are we to be moral?' A strange title! My first thoughts were simple. Of course I am free to make up my own mind about moral issues. I have a conscience and I follow the Gospel because I have chosen to. But on second thoughts it was not that simple.

I am actually conditioned by my parents' attitudes and faith, by my education, by society, by my friends, by the press . . . I could go on. I ended up asking if I am really free at all. Take a very ordinary example. I grew up in a North London family that loved football and supported Tottenham. No amount of persuasion or will-power or even admiration of footballing skills can change my feelings on a Saturday afternoon if Arsenal win and Tottenham lose. I don't seem to be free to be impartial. If I am like this over football, who is to say that I am not equally prejudiced in making moral decisions? Am I ever able to be free?

I suspect most of us conform to what is expected of us without giving it much thought. To challenge the *status quo* takes courage or a strong personality. I was reflecting recently that our daughter, Blanca, certainly has the latter. I came across a note I made when she was hardly four years old. (I used to write down such little anecdotes.) A conversation with her went like this:

Me: Blanca, please don't leave your doll and all her bits and pieces on the floor. They'll only get trodden on.

SILENCE

Me: Blanca, did you hear me? Pick your things up and put them away. You'll get really cross if they get broken.

Blanca: Mummy, I don't *have* to do what you say.

Me: Why not?

Blanca: Because I'm *me*.

I'm very proud of Blanca because she has remained fiercely deter-mined and her very own person. She isn't easily influenced by her peers or by expected behaviour. Having such a strong will can be difficult. It could so easily lead to disaster. It is really costly for Blanca to stand out and act independently. It is much easier to do 'what I'm told to do'.

We older Christians may need shaking up a bit. Even conforming to established Church practice could be an easy 'cop-out'. It takes courage to read the Gospel texts and accept the consequence of what God's Word is actually saying to us. Many of the saints were considered to be quite mad when they acted on what they read.

Francis embraced absolute poverty to the dismay of his rich father. Thomas Aquinas horrified his family when he joined the straggly band of preaching friars. 'They must be mad,' said everyone.

Quite right! In the words of Zorba the Greek, one needs a little madness in order to cut the ropes and be free.

Summary

Advent is a time to look forward to something that happened in the past. This seems the wrong way round. But the freedom God brought about in the past, through his Son, is worked out through us. Its completion is promised for the future. The kingdom of God, proclaimed by Jesus, is the liberation he said was 'near at hand'. Christians believe that people already live in the kingdom of God when they act in a God-like way – in love, forgiveness and compassion. Wherever there is oppression, suffering, injustice and lack of peace, God's kingdom has not yet come. Advent is a time to reflect on what this means. Each one of us is capable of making that kingdom come more quickly. But it is a costly challenge. We may have to give up old ties, old opinions, old 'certainties'. What fools we might look! But it 'needs a little madness to cut the rope and be free'.

He's sent me to give the Good News to the poor,
tell prisoners that they are prisoners no more,
tell blind people that they can see,
and set the downtrodden free.

Give me your tired,
your poor,
your huddled masses
yearning to breathe free,
the wretched refuse
of your teeming shore.
Send these, the homeless,
tempest-tost to me.
I lift my lamp beside
the golden door.

Emma Lazarus, 1883

(These words are inscribed in the base of the Statue of Liberty in New York harbour. They are taken from Emma's poem *The New Colossus* which was inspired by the mass exodus of Jewish refugees from Russia in the 1880s.)

Christ set us free,
   so that we should remain free.
Stand firm, then,
   and do not let yourselves be fastened again
   to the yoke of slavery . . .
You were called to be free,
   do not use your freedom as an opening for self-indulgence,
   but be servants to one another in love,
   since the whole of the Law is summarised
   in the one commandment:
   You must love your neighbour as yourself.

Galatians 5:1, 13-14

Christ has no body on earth but yours,
no hands but yours, no feet but yours.
Yours are the eyes through which his compassion
must look out on the world.

St Teresa of Avila

Questions for discussion

1. How free do you think you really are?

2. Name ten situations in the world today (local or distant) where freedom is denied to people. Do you feel a responsibility to do anything about it? If it's not your responsibility, whose is it?

3. Think of a situation where you experienced or witnessed an act of compassion which you felt brought you into the presence of God. Was God really present?

4. Are there any old 'certainties' that you have ever questioned? What would encourage you to move forward into something new?
   (a) Conviction that the Gospel demands such boldness?
   (b) Support of a community that has already shown a willingness to change?
   (c) Nothing. Old 'certainties' cannot be shaken. They are grounded on faith?

Prayer

O thou who art the light of the minds that know thee,
the life of the souls that love thee,
and the strength of the wills that serve thee:
help us to know thee that we may truly love thee,
and so to love thee that we may fully serve thee,
whom to serve is perfect freedom.
Amen.

Prayer of St Augustine of Hippo, 354-430

The crooked shall be made straight, and the rough places plain

Week Two _____

_____ *Prepare a way for the Lord*

Reading for the second Sunday of Advent

In the fifteenth year of Tiberius Caesar's reign, when Pontius Pilate was governor of Judaea, Herod tetrarch of Galilee, his brother Philip tetrarch of the lands of Ituraea and Trachonitis, Lysanias tetrarch of Abilene, during the pontificate of Annas and Caiaphas, the word of God came to John son of Zechariah, in the wilderness. He went through the whole Jordan district proclaiming a baptism of repentance for the forgiveness of sins, as it is written in the book of the sayings of the prophet Isaiah:

'A voice cries in the wilderness:
Prepare a way for the Lord,
make his paths straight.
Every valley will be filled in,
every mountain and hill be laid low,
winding ways will be straightened
and rough roads made smooth.
And all humanity shall see the salvation of God.'

Luke 3:1-6

Last week we looked at the reassuring words of Jesus:

'Your liberation *is* within reach. Take courage. Hold your heads high!' But, full of hope as we are (are we?), there's still work to be done.

So this week Jesus hands us over to John the Baptist to tell us what it is:

'Prepare a way for the Lord. Make his paths straight.'

A way. A path. A road.

John is using the language of arterial road-building.

In his day, when the Roman Emperor was on a journey to visit one of his provinces (especially the distant ones), a road-building programme had to be set up.

What sort of a road do you need for an imperial coach and horses and a bodyguard?

How wide? How deep? How level? How straight? How solid?

How much uneven ground had to be levelled off?

What ditches needed filling? Or bridges building if the ditch was too wide?

What bends had to be straightened out?

What humps had to be cut through?

What obstacles had to be removed?

What rubbish needed to be carted away?

Do you know Handel's *Messiah*?

Handel turned today's Gospel reading into one of his finest arias:

'Every valley shall be exalted
and every mountain and hill shall be made low,
and the crooked shall be made straight,
and the rough places plain.
and the glory of the Lord shall be revealed.'

Well, how's that for an Advent programme?

Life is a road on which we meet God.

What sort of a road-building programme do I need?

What is too narrow about my life that needs to be widened if God is ever going to make his way to me? My education? My interests? My reading? My circle of friends?

What is so shallow and shaky in my life that it would never bear the weight of a bike, let alone a coach and horses?

What is so devious and crooked that it could do with some straightening out?

What are the ditches and gaps in my life that need a bridge if there's going to be any real communication?
What is the rubbish in my life that needs scrapping?
What is missing in my life that makes it difficult for God to get to me? Not many of us pretend we've got a hotline to God, but we'll have no line to him at all if we've disconnected ourselves.

And of course these questions I've put to myself have to be asked about all my brothers and sisters across the world.
What is thin and shallow and crooked and broken and cluttered about their lives that we could do something about?
Their lines of communication with God are also endangered.

The King is on his way.
No road, no arrival.
If we don't do some road-building this Advent, he can't come to us at Christmas.
It's up to us.

> Our Father who art in heaven,
> thy kingdom come
> thy will be done.

A voice cries in the wilderness:
Prepare a way for the Lord, make his paths straight.

How do we make paths straight?

John the Baptist used the roadways as a symbol. I was thinking about this symbolism when I came across the notes I wrote about our children many years ago. (I mentioned them last week.) This little story about Pedro is so charming I thought I would share it. It is not precisely about roads, but never mind! This is how I wrote up the incident.

Pedro gave me a fright last night. He had been sneezing a bit and complaining of a 'funny nose'. A warm bath, a cuddle and early bed seemed a good idea. His energy revived with the splashing about in the water with Blanca. Before they cleaned their teeth (done in the bath so I can keep track of the toothbrushes) I gave Pedro a dose of Calpol.

But Blanca chose the very moment that Pedro was swallowing to splash him in the face. He gulped and choked. The medicine went down the wrong way and the poor little fellow couldn't get his breath. He was very frightened and so was I. A quiet boy went to bed, less enthusiastic than usual about the bedtime story.

In the morning he still seemed subdued and sat, untypically, waiting quietly for his breakfast. Then I noticed he was chewing his cornflakes with great deliberation and swallowing carefully. Oh dear, was he all right?

Suddenly, with a broad grin and his usual cheer he said, 'Mummy, I've got a roundabout in my mouth and I'm telling the cornflakes to go round it and then off along the right road!' How brilliant. My little boy knows how to solve his own problems.

Three-year-old Pedro loved his cars and made roadway systems across the kitchen floor. As his collection grew, the roads stretched down the hallway. He knew all about roundabouts and traffic lights, T-junctions and dual carriageways. John the Baptist probably only knew small, local, unpaved roads and the great Roman highways. The latter were impressive and important. We certainly need to recognise the significance of symbols used in the Gospels because the images usually only fit into the contemporary context. Long, wide, straight highways today are, for many of us, uninspiring, boring motorways. Give me, any time, a winding, quiet, unimportant country road!

Perhaps a Palestinian Ermine Street or Watling Street was under construction when John was preaching. Perhaps, he had simply been reading his Scriptures; he was quoting from the Book of Isaiah. It might help us to go right round the roundabout and back to the prophet who dreamed up this arterial road.

Isaiah is probably the best known of the prophets. Certainly he is the most outstanding one. From 740 to 690 BC Isaiah preached of a God of transcendence and holiness. God was the master of history who asked for his people's faith and absolute trust. But Assyria was expanding towards Egypt at this time and had conquered the northern kingdom of Israel. The people in the southern kingdom of Judah were tempted to use political, military means to protect its borders. Isaiah protested. His name actually spelt out his message. It means 'Salvation comes from Yahweh', not from armies.

The words quoted by John the Baptist, however, come from the second part of the Book of Isaiah. These chapters were added some 150 years later by disciples of the great prophet. By this time Isaiah's dire warnings had become fact. Judah had fallen to invading armies and the people had become exiles in Babylon. Second Isaiah, or the Book of Consolation, is a dramatic presentation of Israel placing itself completely in God's hands, ready at last to be rescued from slavery.

John the Baptist took his words from the opening lines of Second Isaiah, who looks forward to the coming of God, like a king, through the Arabian desert, to lead his exiled people home to Jerusalem.

A voice cries, 'Prepare in the desert
a way for Yahweh.
Make a straight highway for our God
across the wastelands.

Let every valley be filled in,
every mountain and hill be levelled,
every cliff become a plateau,
every escarpment a plain;
then the glory of Yahweh will be revealed
and all humanity will see it together,
for the mouth of Yahweh has spoken.'
Isaiah 40:3-5

What actually is a prophecy? All too often in school I found that pupils presumed that prophets had been 'told' by God details about the future coming of Jesus. They presumed too that Jesus knew he was the fulfilment of these prophecies and that he set out to fulfil them, one by one. Biblical scholars will tell us that it is not like that at all. Bert describes it this way:

A prophecy is not a prediction which God and people are forced to follow; it is not an absolute and determining outside force. It is an insight into a situation, stating what will result if people continue in a certain way. It is given either to persuade people to change or to encourage people to remain faithful.

Isaiah's disciples were not consciously predicting the coming of Jesus. They were offering consolation to the exiles in Babylon, offering them the hope that Babylon had had its day, and a new exodus was coming that would see the people return to a revived Jerusalem. But paths needed straightening out; the road to Jerusalem was beckoning. It is difficult to underestimate the importance of Jerusalem for the Jews. 'Next year in Jerusalem.' It was going to become a pretty important place for Christians too. (And for Muslims later on.)

Luke has recognised this. Why not take some time this Advent to browse through his Gospel, bearing in mind journeys and Jerusalem? Notice particularly chapters 9 to 19. The section is set within the framework of the journey towards Jerusalem. The goal for Jesus is to reach that city. At least ten times we read the signpost: 'towards Jerusalem'. The road was not a straight highway; it is left deliberately vague as Jesus preached along the way, going through towns and villages. But what *is* straight, direct and focused is Jesus' determination to reach Jerusalem for his Passover. Luke even gives us a hint of this 'journey to Jerusalem' theme in the introduction to the Gospel when he writes of the boy Jesus staying in Jerusalem, at the expense of his fretting parents.

As I am writing this, Pope John Paul II, in spite of ill health, is following Jesus' footsteps through the Holy Land. He had determined to make this pilgrimage to celebrate the millennium. On his arrival, three children held out a bowl of soil for him to bless. The children were Jewish, Christian and Muslim. I think Luke would have been delighted at the gesture. He, of all the New Testament writers, had a vision of universality. He wanted the Good News to reach all peoples. Mark and Matthew finish the Isaiah quotation at verse 40, but Luke continues to include the promise of universal salvation in the New Jerusalem:

. . . then the glory of Yahweh will be revealed,
and all humanity will see it together.

Advent is a wonderful time to look forward in hope to a future when all humanity will recognise the glory of God, and so live in harmony. It was a very early saint, St Irenaeus, who described the glory of God as 'a person fully human'. He surely meant us to see in the human Jesus the very face of God. But he also meant us to recognise the glory of God in the face of every human being. This is why the great prophets of old and the prophets of today cry out against human injustice and abuse. Martin Luther King, Nelson Mandela and Desmond Tutu, for example, who are voices for the black peoples who have been denied their freedom. And Archbishop Oscar Romero and Archbishop Hélder Câmara, who are voices for the poor who are exploited by rich governments. We will look at this next week.

Meanwhile, this week, let's go on a spiritual pilgrimage to 'Jerusalem', finding in our Gospel reading the promise of a New Jerusalem. It lies at the end of the road and Jesus will accompany us along the way – if we wish.

Summary

John the Baptist, a voice in the wilderness, proclaimed, 'Prepare a way for the Lord, make his paths straight.' He calls for valleys to be infilled, mountains broken down and the land straightened out for the coming of the Lord. We are preparing for Christ's coming and it would be a useful exercise for us to consider what needs putting straight in our own lives before he comes. We can look at the 'straight road' symbol in another way. John was quoting from the Book of Isaiah which had protested that the People of God were tempted to seek political solutions to their problems, when 'Salvation comes from Yahweh'. The prophets, including John, spoke to their contemporaries, offering comfort and hope in a better future. They directed their people towards Jerusalem, where Jesus himself would one day celebrate his Passover. Christians today are on a pilgrimage towards the New Jerusalem. Jesus can accompany us on this road, if we let him.

Experience teaches us that love does not consist in looking another in the eye; rather in looking outward together in the same direction.

Antoine de Saint-Exupery, 1900-1944

Lead, kindly Light, amid th'encircling gloom, lead thou me on;
the night is dark, and I am far from home, lead thou me on.
Keep thou my feet; I do not ask to see
the distant scene; one step enough for me.

I was not ever thus, nor prayed that thou shouldst lead me on;
I loved to choose and see my path, but now lead thou me on.
I loved the garish day, and, spite of fears,
pride ruled my will: remember not past years.

So long thy pow'r hath blest me, sure it still will lead me on
o'er moor and fen, o'er crag and torrent till the night is gone.
And with the morn those angel faces smile,
which I have loved long since and lost awhile.

John Henry Newman, 1801-1890

The road to Christian unity is like a road with no exit, a pilgrimage
of grace we make together.

Archbishop Cormac Murphy O'Connor

Jerusalem the golden,
with milk and honey blest,
beneath thy contemplation
sink heart and voice oppressed.
I know not, oh, I know not
what joys await us there,
what radiancy of glory,
what bliss beyond compare.

O sweet and blessed country,
the home of God's elect!
O sweet and blessed country
that eager hearts expect!
Jesus, in mercy bring us
to that dear land of rest;
who art, with God the Father
and Spirit, ever blest.

Bernard of Cluny (12th century), translated by J. M. Neale, d. 1866

He who would valiant be
'gainst all disaster,
let him in constancy
follow the Master.

There's no discouragement
shall make him once relent
his first avowed intent
to be a pilgrim.

Since, Lord, thou dost defend
us with thy Spirit,
we know we at the end
shall life inherit.
Then fancies flee away!
I'll fear not what men say
I'll labour night and day
to be a pilgrim.

Percy Dearmer after John Bunyan, 1628-1688

Questions for discussion

1. Read Archbishop Murphy O'Connor's words (on page 32) about unity.

   (a) What does he mean when he says that this road has no exit?

   (b) Where is the road leading?

2. Will 'all humanity live together in harmony' one day? Would it be more realistic to say that Islam, Judaism and Christianity meet together, occasionally, at a roundabout and then all go off in different directions?

3. Find references in Luke's Gospel to journeys. Share your findings if you are in a group. Can you see any pattern in Luke's Gospel?

4. Who would you consider to be today's prophets? Why? Why are so many recognised 'prophets' male? (Or are we not seeing the female ones?)

Prayer

I rejoiced that they said to me,
'Let us go to the house of Yahweh.'
At last our feet are standing
at your gates, Jerusalem. . . .

Pray for the peace of Jerusalem,
prosperity for your homes!
Peace within your walls,
prosperity in your palaces!

For love of my brethren and my friends
I will say, 'Peace upon you!'
For love of the house of Yahweh our God
I will pray for your well-being.

Psalm 122

UNWRA photograph

Are you ready?

Week Three

Are you ready?

Reading for the third Sunday of Advent

When all the people asked John, 'What must we do, then?' he answered, 'If anyone has two tunics he must share with the man who has none, and the one with something to eat must do the same.' There were tax collectors too who came for baptism, and these said to him, 'Master, what must we do?' He said to them, 'Exact no more than your rate.' Some soldiers asked him in their turn, **'What about us? What must we do?' He said to them, 'No intimidation! No extortion! Be content with your pay!'**

Luke 3:10-18

This week John the Baptist continues to face us.

He's a pretty ferocious figure, and if you look at the whole of today's Gospel reading, you'll agree that you wouldn't want him preaching his hellfire sermon from your pulpit!

But the audience he's addressing on this page of the Gospel is a group of the Roman occupation army that was happening by, and like most mercenary soldiers they could be real thugs.

They were only in the army for the money, and intimidation, extortion and inflation were their stock in trade.

A friend of ours tried to put this piece of the Gospel into modern terms:

Armed Forces, Police, Prison Officers –
yours is a dangerous vocation!
Resist the temptation to take pleasure in violence.
Be in the front line of the genuine peace marches,
marching with the people, not against them.
Don't trade in your consciences for a quiet life and fat pensions!

Jose Luis Cortes, translated by John Medcalf

So we don't need to worry overmuch about the ban John the Baptist is putting on pay rises.

He's talking to extortioners, not to people being *exploited* by extortioners, working for peanuts in the sweatshops of the world.

But John has a word for us too: 'Don't'.

He told us last week what we ought to be doing to prepare for the coming of God.

Today he's telling us what we ought to *stop* doing.

What does he have in mind?

What is there in my life that needs changing?

What ought I to stop doing that's blocking God's coming into our world?

How, for instance, can I stop being as selfish and self-centred as I am?

Am I aware of the needs even of those who are close to me? People are for loving, not for using.

How should I stop thinking of other people as none of my concern – or, worse, as rivals that I've got to do down – instead of as my brothers and sisters?

Do I patronise or even make fun of people less well off than myself, or less fortunate, or less able? In what way can I stop demeaning them in my eyes?

When the papers or TV tell me, day after day, about the world's tragedies, wars, disasters, suffering and deprivation, do I just shrug and say, 'There's nothing I can do about it', instead of asking, 'What can I do about it?' How about a bit of compassion, instead of my habitual unconcern?

Does it ever worry me that well over half of the human race lives at bare subsistence level? Has the capitalist mindset I've grown up with so blinded and deafened me that I can no longer see them or hear their cry of fair shares for all, not just for a few?

On a smaller scale, how much cheating, fiddling, skiving, free-riding and general dishonesty is there in my life? Could I put a stop to it – at least for Advent?

Advent, like Lent, is a time for giving up things.
What could I stop doing, at least for a bit, to allow God into my life?
It needn't disrupt my life totally: it might even improve it.
Perhaps I should ask myself whether people, when they see me coming, say, 'Oh good' or 'Oh God'.
What should I stop doing to make them change?

Obviously this doesn't mean we have only a few days left to become saints.
The wise old St Benedict, when he was composing a set of rules for his Benedictine monks to live by, wrote:
'People say that monks should never drink wine.
If I made that a rule, I wouldn't have any monks.
So we'll just say: Wine in moderation.'

We become saints slowly.

Our Father, who art in heaven,
thy kingdom come,
thy will be done.
Forgive us our trespasses.

'What about us? What must we do?'
John the Baptist said to them: 'No intimidation! No extortion!
Be content with your pay!'

Be content with your pay

I was watching *Question Time* last night and it struck me that John the Baptist would make a marvellous member of the panel. He would give people a run for their money! I was shocked (and so were some members of the audience and the panel) at the bitter, prejudiced attitudes of some of the audience. They were scathing in their attack on the refugees coming into the country from the impoverished and war-torn countries of Eastern Europe. They seemed full of hatred for anyone whose needs may affect their life in any way. It was a very sad spectacle. It needed some straight talking from a fiery John the Baptist.

Thank God there are modern-day prophets who remind us of our responsibilities for each other. And I thank God that we have a government that offers sanctuary to people in need. If we are asking ourselves this Advent how we should personally respond to John's admonition, 'Be content with your pay', perhaps we could look around the world and get things into perspective.

As a family we are rather privileged to have had the opportunity to do just that.

At the very time we were preparing to go to Colombia to adopt our children we noticed an article in the Catholic press about a Colombian Jesuit priest, Father Carlos Vasco. He was living in a shanty town at the edge of Bogota. He was also professor of mathematics at the Jesuit university. We resolved to visit him. With difficulty we found him in his small hut in the midst of his 'barrio' community. The crowded dwellings, made from building site throwaways, nestled into the side of the hill. It was a shock to see so close together the affluence of the wealthy Colombians who enjoyed the normal features of city life and the total poverty of the displaced 'barrio' dwellers. As we crossed the road from the city, we left behind pleasant buildings, elegant hotels, good pavements, electricity, water, shops and adequate transport. On the other side of the road everything was missing.

Shanty town dwellers have no mains water, no electricity, no roads and drainage, no sanitation, no shops, no health facilities.

Father Carlos had managed to divert a meagre water supply and to tap into a little electricity from across the road. He and his community had also managed to 'acquire' enough bricks from city building works to build a community room which also served as a school. Bert and I were left stunned by the dignity and patience of these poor people. When we asked Father Carlos how they survived such poverty, he explained that some men managed to get seasonal jobs on the building sites and some of the women worked as domestics in the hotels. 'What about those who can't work?' we asked. 'Well, of course,' he replied, 'their neighbours will share what they earn with them. People here will always help each other.'

When we returned to England it was to find that the teaching profession was organising its first major strike for higher pay. I was so glad that I was leaving the classroom to be a full-time mother to our Colombian twins. I could not have taken part in the protest, not after what we had seen. Lest you should think that our experience was not typical, here is what Mother Teresa of Calcutta once witnessed:

> Some weeks back I heard there was a family that had not eaten for some days – a Hindu family – so I took some rice and I went to the family. Before I knew where I was, the mother of the family had divided the rice into two and she took the other half to the next-door neighbours, who happened to be a Muslim family. Then I asked her, 'How much will all of you have to share? There are already ten of you with that bit of rice.' The mother replied, 'They have not eaten either.'

I felt angry with those in the television audience who were so insensitive to the plight of the desperate poor. Mother Teresa was more understanding. She once said, 'The trouble is that rich people, well-to-do people, very often don't really know who the poor are; and that is why we can forgive them, for knowledge can only lead to love, and love to service. And so, if they are not touched by them, it's because they do not know them.' This is our dilemma in our rich, first world.

This first came home to me at the time of the Vietnamese boat people. I was teaching at the time. A local Anglican priest and his family made the extraordinarily generous offer of using their life savings to buy a house for a refugee family. I was happy to provide some extra hands from my class of fourteen-year-olds to help prepare the house for their arrival. When the family had settled in, we welcomed them with a 'party' held in our classroom, during RE time.

Some months later we were discussing prejudice in class. To my dismay some of the pupils took a very negative view towards refugees. 'Those foreigners who come over here and take our jobs,' they said. 'You mean the boat people,' I said. There was a silence, followed by a hesitant voice: 'Well, no, not them, they are different.' The lesson then took a different turn. As one girl put it, 'We know our family, by name. They are delightful and we would never want to send them back.' We concluded that it is easy to judge 'them' and to feel threatened by 'them'. But when 'them' become real people with weary and troubled eyes – grandma who was almost blind with cataracts, undernourished children who could hardly believe it when they were offered sweets and toys, and gentle parents speechless with wonder at the generosity of their host family – then it is quite a different matter. We care about people we know.

When John asked those soldiers to 'Be content with your pay', he also exhorted the crowds to share all they had with the poor: 'Anyone who has two tunics must share with the one who has none, and anyone with something to eat must do the same.' The Anglican priest and his family did just that. Amazing! It is a rare response to the Gospel. Most of us are content to contribute to CAFOD, Christian Aid or UNICEF, and buy the odd copy of *The Big Issue*.

It really isn't easy to escape the materialism of our 'rich', democratic social background. How can we have any empathy with refugees who flee from a poverty or brutality that is simply un-known in our country? All *we* know is the repeated promises made by successive governments of better healthcare, better education, higher wages and adequate pensions. I don't think John the Baptist would be heard if he cried out, just before an election, 'Be content with your pay, and if you have two of anything give one away to the poor.' We have been conditioned to accumulate wealth. So, in addition to what we earn, we want to win the lottery and become millionaires. It is clearly much more of a challenge to live the Gospel in comfortable Britain than in Vietnam, El Salvador or Mozambique.

Centuries ago John Wesley was aware of the problem of wealth for Christians who enjoy a settled economy. He encouraged them to 'gain all you can; save all you can; give all you can'. He practised what he preached. He came into some wealth from his published writings, but at his death his total possessions were two silver spoons and a few pounds.

We can't ignore the preaching of John the Baptist this Advent, nor the example of prophets like Romero, Wesley or Mother Teresa. How can we ordinary Christians respond in a practical way? Clearly we are not all expected to give half of the contents of our homes away? *Are we?* Maybe it is our voices that should be heard? Archbishop Romero did not sell up his residence and choose to live in a hovel, but he spoke out with such insistence on the rights of the dispossessed that his opponents shot him, to silence him.

Maybe our voices could be heard in the defence of the refugees and the homeless in Britain. Parts of the press are excelling themselves in bad-mouthing them and claiming that the country is becoming a soft touch for gypsies and economic migrants. 'They are abusing our system,' they say. Mary and Joseph were refugees. Shouldn't we urge our government to stand by today's refugees and offer them at least a stable?

Summary

The rather ferocious John the Baptist tells us this week what we should and shouldn't do in preparation for the coming of God. John is particularly fierce with members of the Roman occupation army who were in the job for money, extortion and intimidation. He told them to be content with their pay. He urged everyone to share what they owned with the poor. Advent is a good time for us to look closely at our attitudes to wealth and material goods. The indications are that our capitalist mindset blinds and deafens us: we can no longer see the destitute or hear the cries of the needy. If it is not practical for us to share our goods with others, perhaps we should follow the example of recent prophets, like Archbishop Romero, and speak out for the poor. In our country today these poor are the displaced refugees who receive as much abuse as welcome. Can we change this?

You will not cheat the poor among you of their rights at law. Keep clear of fraud. You will accept no bribes, for a bribe blinds the clear-sighted and is the ruin of the cause of the upright. You will not oppress the alien; you know how an alien feels, for you yourselves were once aliens in Egypt.

Exodus 23:6-9

Open our eyes, Lord,
  to see the needs around us,
  especially the needs of refugees
  who have come to us for shelter and hope.

Open our ears, Lord,
  to hear what you are saying to us
  through the words of John the Baptist;
  through today's prophets and through the people we meet.

Open our lips, Lord,
    to tell others the Good News of the Gospel
    that you are coming to save the poor, the blind,
    the imprisoned and the homeless.

Open our hands, Lord,
    to do your work for those in need,
    because you have no other hands but ours.

Open our minds, Lord,
    to discover new truths about you and about ourselves,
    about your generosity and about our greed.

Open our hearts, Lord,
    to welcome you with love,
    in the lives and needs of our neighbours.

Prepare ye the way of the Lord.
Prepare ye the way of the Lord.
Prepare ye the way of the Lord.
Prepare ye the way of the Lord.

(Play the music and/or sing the words as in the musical *Godspell*).

Questions for discussion

1. If we had a John the Baptist preaching in Britain today, what are the issues he would be most ferocious about?

2. Is it the role of Church authority to challenge governments and institutions that seek to make the rich become richer, if this implies that the poor become poorer?

3. Mary and Joseph were refugees. In what way could we show respect and offer hospitality to the refugees in our country today?

4. List the ways we could use our 'voices' in support of the poor and marginalised.

Prayer

Watch, dear Lord,
with those who wake, and watch, and weep tonight,
and give your angels charge over those who sleep.
Tend your sick ones, O Lord Christ,
rest your weary ones.
Soothe your suffering ones.
Pity your afflicted ones.
Shield your joyous ones,
And all for your love's sake,
Amen.

St Augustine of Hippo, 354-430

UNWRA photograph

Mary homeless in Bethlehem

Week Four

God keeps his promise

Reading for the fourth Sunday of Advent

Mary set out at that time and went as quickly as she could to a town in the hill country of Judah. She went into Zechariah's house and greeted Elizabeth. Now as soon as Elizabeth heard Mary's greeting, the child leapt in her womb and Elizabeth was filled with the Holy Spirit. She gave a loud cry and said, 'Of all women you are the most blessed, and blessed is the fruit of your womb. Why should I be honoured with a visit from the mother of my Lord? For the moment your greeting reached my ears, the child in my womb leapt for joy. Yes, **blessed is she who believed that the promise made her by the Lord would be fulfilled**.'

Luke 1:39-45

So, we're nearly at the end of our Advent preparation for Christmas. The promise made to us over and over again is now going to be fulfilled.

What is perhaps rather surprising about the reading for this last Sunday of Advent is its utter contrast with the first three Sundays.

The word 'Advent', as we saw, means arriving or coming.

This season of Advent has been about the coming of God, and in the readings of all the last three Sundays, that coming has been presented as a pretty breathtaking event, frightening perhaps – you could even say threatening.

The God who comes, and now stands at the threshold, so we've been told, is a king, a judge, a warrior, a liberator. (Gracious! What's he going to liberate me from?)

But as we come to the end of this season, and peep through the door on this last week of Advent, we see it's only a baby!

A baby! How lovely! How sweet!
Who can resist cooing over a baby in its crib?
This doesn't frighten me at all!
What? A baby? Threaten me? No way!

Very true.
But perhaps we're looking at the whole thing back to front.
The question is not: Does the baby pose a threat to me?
The question is: Do I pose a threat to the baby?

The whole of Advent has been about how God can come more
deeply and more effectively into our lives.
All of us came into the world as babies.
If God is going to come into our world, that's the only way there
is: as a baby.
And a baby doesn't threaten us. God does not threaten us.
It's the other way round. It's the violent and aggressive people we've
grown into that threaten God.
A newborn baby can't hate, or fight, or kill.
Neither does God. In a sense, he's as helpless as a baby.
It's up to you and me whether we let him grow.

And notice how in this Sunday's Gospel reading Mary is presented in exactly the same way.
She comes into the story in exactly the same context of littleness, of
defencelessness, of nothingness.
She too knows that she is as helpless as a baby.
And it's only through people who have emptied themselves out in
this way that God can come into the world.
God comes into the world in people who want to be so little that
they're no longer a threat to anyone.

He looks on his servant in her nothingness
Henceforth all ages will call me blessed.
He cast the mighty from their thrones
and raises the lowly.

Luke 1:47-52 (Grail translation)

It isn't the powerful and mighty, the violent and strong, who bring
    God into the world.
It's people like Mary.

Mary the slum-dweller
Mary who longed for the liberation of her people
Mary who sang to God of the poor
Mary homeless in Bethlehem
Mary exiled from her native land
Mary pilgrim with her people
Blessed are you among women.
Noticias Aliadas

Hail Mary, full of grace,
the Lord is with thee.
Blessed art thou among women.

*Elizabeth said to Mary: 'Blessed is she who has believed
that the promise made her by the Lord would be fulfilled.'*

Of all women you are the most blessed

There is nothing quite like reflecting on the birth of Jesus in Bethlehem itself. Anyone who has visited the Holy Land will tell you what an extraordinary experience it is. Places don't exactly look like scenes on the Christmas cards – Bethlehem is built-up and dominated by the great Basilica of the Nativity. As pilgrims enter the town they are greeted by a banner across the road which says, in Hebrew, 'Beruchim Habaim – Blessed is he who comes'. Underneath, in Arabic, the welcome reads, 'Ahalan vesahalan – My tent is yours.'

The basilica was built over 1,600 years ago over the cave which had been venerated by the early Christians as the place of the birth of Jesus. The Crusaders had to rescue the church from the Saracens in the Middle Ages. To stop the Saracen soldiers riding into the building on horseback the door was walled up. Even today the only entrance is the small postern gate, to the side of the building. Everyone has to bend low – to avoid banging their heads – to enter this sacred place. Pilgrims have to bend double again when they approach the little chapel at the end of the church, to go down steps to the cave cut into the rock. Beneath an altar in the cave is a silver star set into the ground. It bears the inscription, 'Here, of the virgin Mary, was born Jesus Christ.'

In a broadcast for the BBC that Bert once made from Bethlehem, he said:

> It's a sort of parable, I've always thought when I've visited Bethlehem, that no one can come and see the place where Jesus was born without making this act of humility and obeisance. It's as if the very stones are saying to you, 'You've got to stoop here, pilgrim, this place where God has stooped so low for you.'

It is an amazing thought that the birth of Jesus celebrates a reversal of roles. God, the supreme Mystery, the Creator of all things, the transcendent, the Holy One who welcomes us as his children and heirs to his kingdom, allows the tables to be turned here in Bethlehem.

The birth of Jesus means that ordinary, everyday, little people, like you and me, turn to God and say, 'Ahalan vesahalan – My tent is your tent.' Mary was the first to say those words and Christians have followed her example ever since. Advent is the time to welcome the indescribable mystery which we call God, to come and dwell with us. 'O come, O come, Emmanuel.'

The whole mystery of the Incarnation never fails to amaze me. The beauty of this most fundamental doctrine of our faith is that it roots the presence of God firmly in our world of everyday life. We don't have to look into the heavens, or wait for an after-life to meet God personally! And that presence of God is often a surprise, a welcome ray of light into a very ordinary, often tiring and un-eventful day. In my written record of my early days as a mother I once reflected on the enormity of this Christian belief. Here is what I wrote down.

I was on the floor in Marks and Spencers measuring up a pair of trousers on Pedro, when I suddenly saw, more clearly than ever before, the world as he sees it. It was most uncomfortable at that moment. Sales shoppers don't stop for little boys. Swinging shoulder bags missed our ears by inches. Bulging shopping baskets didn't miss. But worst of all was the mass of legs and arms with hardly any faces that pressed in upon us with claustrophobic effect.

No wonder the children don't always enjoy shopping with me. No wonder they complain and want to get back home. It isn't so much that they can't reach the counters to see what I am looking at, it is this awful feeling of being beneath the adults, of being lowly and disadvantaged. Height gives power, I thought to myself as I paid for the trousers.

Blanca was saying the other day that 'God is up in heaven'. This is a new language in our household, introduced now from school. Pedro is convinced that God lives up in the moon. I wonder if this lofty height gives God more threatening power in their eyes. I hope it won't make them see him as remote.

As every parent knows, the happiest moments are often spent on the floor with the children, playing trains or building Lego. They love to climb on top of us to establish that they have power too. As Blanca knelt on my lap this evening, combing my hair – and my eyebrows – I thought how good it is that the Christian doctrine of Incarnation tells us to look for God here at eye level, and not high up in the skies.

Sixteen years on and I still marvel at the Christmas message of *God with us.* We have gone on building churches and great basilicas, like the one in Bethlehem – which is very nice – but the event that brings an unending flow of pilgrims to the little town is actually saying that God is present *in* the world of ordinary people. A friend of ours, Eamon Duffy, expressed this truth perfectly in these words:

At the heart of Christianity is the insistence that all our ex-perience is religious, or none of it is. The Incarnation points us away from a God locked into the sacred, towards One who informs all that we do and are, to be encountered most fully not merely and not most in the temple or the prayer room, but in the faces of our fellow men and women; the God not of our souls, but of our whole humanity. We need to be aware of being too spiritual.

The same reality was clearly in the mind of the foundress of the Little Sisters of Jesus. Sister Magdeleine had some difficulty at first in persuading Vatican authorities to recognise her vision for her communities. Some people in Rome said it was hardly worthy of a religious sister to carry a knapsack, travel like the poor, and be nursed in open hospital wards with local people. She had given this advice to her sisters: 'Before being religious, be *human* and Christian.' This sounded quite radical in the 1940s, but the Pope and his advisers recognised the truth of her life and her humility by giving official approval to everything she requested.

As Advent draws to a close and the Christmas lights begin to flicker, our final meditation can centre on Mary, blessed among women.

Mary the slum-dweller
Mary who longed for the liberation of her people
Mary who sang to God of the poor
Mary homeless in Bethlehem
Mary exiled in Bethlehem
Mary pilgrim with her people
Blessed are you among women.

Noticias Aliadas

I have always been humbled by the way our young people grasp the mystery of the Incarnation and see it as the heart of Christianity. They move from the sacred to the secular world with ease. If they sometimes find Church and doctrinal language difficult to comprehend, they seem to have no problem in grasping the Gospel message. I recently helped organise a school poetry competition for UNICEF. We were wanting to highlight the appalling death-rate of young mothers in the Third World whilst giving birth. One thirteen-year-old, Hannah, quite naturally turned to Mary in her thoughts.

When I think of mothers
I think of Mary, the mother of Jesus.
She was told she was having a baby
when she was very young.
This baby was to be the Son of God.
She must have been very frightened,
she wasn't much more than a child herself,
and God had given her a massive responsibility.
There must have been hundreds of confused thoughts
running through her head,
but she said 'Yes' to God.

Then she and Joseph had to leave Nazareth,
to travel to his home town of Bethlehem.
The journey was long and hard,
all that way on a donkey.
When they finally got to Bethlehem there were no rooms.
They stayed in a stable.
Jesus was born in a cold, dark, dirty stable,
not very good conditions for the Son of God.

Two thousand years later, in places like Africa,
babies are still being born in stables,
on roadsides or on to dirty mud floors.
Let these mothers see Mary as an inspiration.
She had to face the hardships they face;
she knows what they are going through.
Let our Mother, God's Mother,
be there for them whenever they need her.

Hannah Long, age 13, from Notre Dame High School, Norwich

Hannah is in a long line of Christians who think lovingly of Mary and turn to her for inspiration. It may help us in these final days of Advent preparation to turn to some of these poets, and reflect on their words and ways of honouring this most lovely of mothers. My choice is the following hymn:

The angel Gabriel from heaven came,
his wings as drifted snow, his eyes as flame.
'All hail,' said he, 'thou lowly maiden, Mary,
most highly favoured lady, Gloria!'

'For know a blessed mother thou shalt be.
All generations laud and honour thee.
Thy Son shall be Emmanuel, by seers foretold,
most highly favoured lady, Gloria.'

Then gentle Mary meekly bowed her head.
'To me be as it pleaseth God,' she said.
'My soul shall laud and magnify his holy name!'
Most highly favoured lady, Gloria!

Of her, Emmanuel the Christ was born
in Bethlehem, all on a Christmas morn;
and Christian folk throughout the world will ever say:
'Most highly favoured lady, Gloria!'

Sabine Baring-Gould, 1834-1924

Summary

As we near the end of Advent the promise made to us is now to be fulfilled. The amazing thing is that the God who comes does not appear as the great king, judge, warrior or liberator we could have expected, but as a tiny baby. And this helpless baby is born in the most humble of situations – as a refugee in a borrowed stable. It is a fitting parable that the basilica in Bethlehem, where this mystery of the birth of Jesus is celebrated, can only be entered by stooping down. Pilgrims must bend low to greet their Saviour. Mary, the humble girl from Nazareth, was the first to welcome Jesus: 'Ahalan vesahalan – My tent is your tent.' We call this mystery the Incarnation, the astounding news that God is to be found no longer in the heavens but here, on earth in ordinary human events. This is Good News.

Questions for discussion

1. On page 50 Bert wrote, 'It's up to you and me whether we let him (God) grow.' What do you think he means? How can we be responsible for this?

2. Look again at the description of Mary on pages 51 and 55. Relate each 'title' to real situations in the world of the second millennium.

3. 'Ahalan vesahalan – My tent is yours.' If this is the greeting of Bethlehem, how can we make it our greeting to others at Christmas? Is it easy to have open doors? Is it prudent?

4. If the Incarnation means that God is to be found in our ordinary, everyday lives, do we need churches?

5. Try writing your own poem or hymn about Mary.

Prayer

The baker-woman in her humble lodge
received the grain of wheat from God;
for nine whole months the grain she stored:
Behold the handmaid of the Lord.
Make us the bread, Mary, Mary,
make us the bread, we need to be fed.

The baker-woman took the road which led
to Bethlehem, the House of Bread.
To knead the bread she laboured through the night
and brought it forth about midnight.

Bake us the bread, Mary, Mary,
bake us the bread, we need to be fed.

Marie Noel, translated by H. J. Richards

A dissenter's Hail Mary

You bore him, fed him, clothed him, led him;
you carried him, suckled him, sang him to sleep.
You nursed him, enfolded him, encouraged him, scolded him;
you suffered him, moved him to laugh (and to weep).
You were the chosen one, you were the maiden,
he was yours before he was ours.
With your flesh the Word was laden,
Seed of eternity, Hope of the years.
For your obedience, your faith and your firmness,
for your humility, tenderness, grace,
sinners salute you: presume to say 'Thank you',
who love him and serve him
but had not your place.

James Badcock, b. 1915

Conclusion

Today we have finished writing this little book for Advent. This morning Bishop Cormac Murphy-O'Connor was installed as the new Archbishop of Westminster. In his address, outlining his vision and hopes for the future, he spoke movingly of the 'truth of our human condition'. He made it very clear that we are called to work for the freedom of all our sisters and brothers. Some of the themes and ideas we have offered for Advent reflection in these pages were touched upon in his address. So it makes a fitting conclusion to leave you with his words:

Is it not extraordinary that in this age of technological advancement, so many live in dire poverty, while we claim so much of the world's riches? In common witness with fellow Christians, and, indeed, with those of other faiths, and all people of good will, I believe that every one of us is meant to live by what is true, by the very truth of our humanity, the truth of our human condition.

You see, we are not free people when, as individuals or as a society, we live in ways that undermine or deny the truth of how we are meant to live. This truth is fundamentally that every human being has a dignity because made in the image and likeness of God. And that dignity must be protected and nourished above all else.

People forget that the principal goal of the moral life is the flourishing and fulfilment of that humanity for which all of us have been created. The moral question is not, therefore, 'What ought we to do?' – but 'What kind of persons are we called to become?'

Good question!
What kind of persons are we called to become this Advent?

Come, Lord Jesus

Come to us, Lord Jesus Christ,
come as we search the scriptures and see God's hidden purpose,
come as we walk the lonely road, needing a companion,
come when life mystifies and perplexes us,
come into our disappointments and unease,
come at table when we share our food and hopes,
and, coming, open our eyes to recognise you.
Donald Hilton, b. 1932